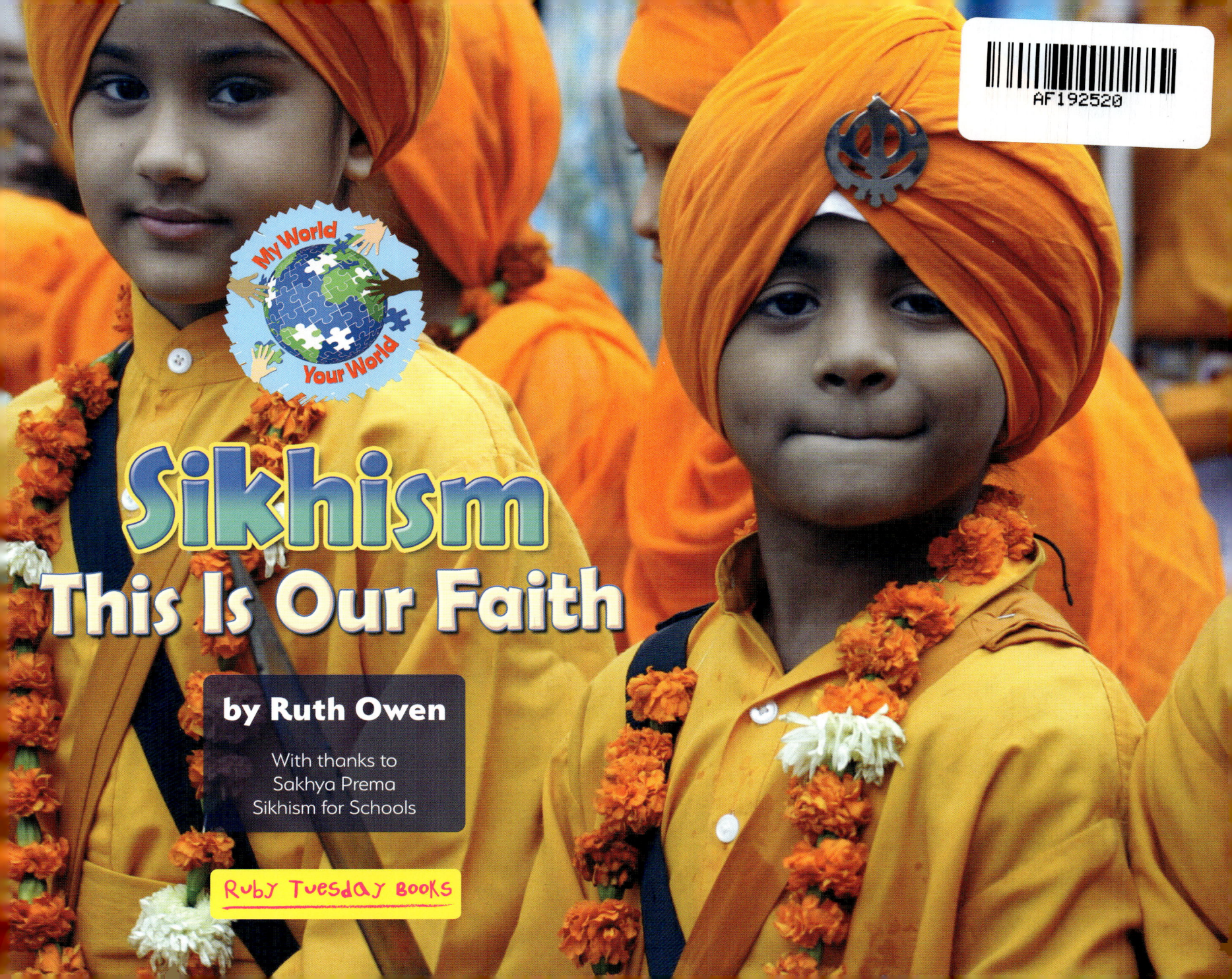

My World Your World

Sikhism
This Is Our Faith

by Ruth Owen

With thanks to
Sakhya Prema
Sikhism for Schools

Ruby Tuesday Books

Published in 2026 by Ruby Tuesday Books Ltd.
Copyright © 2026 Ruby Tuesday Books Ltd.

Editor: Mark J. Sachner
Design & Production: Tammy West

Printed in Malta by Gutenberg Press

Photo Credits:

Alamy: Cover (Keith Larby), 1 (Fredrik Renander), 7 (Richard Levine), 9 (Sajj Maramon), 11T (Jackie Smith), 12L (Imago), 12R (Life's Like That), 13L (World Religions Photo Library), 13R (Kevin Wheal Kent), 14 (Mauritius images GmbH), 15R (Judi Saunders), 16 (Francois-Olivier Dommergues), 17L (Andy Morton), 17R (Michael Wheatley), 19 (Mark Kerrison), 20 (Universal Images Group North America LLC), 21 (Ira Berger), 22 (Ira Berger); Public Domain: 6; Shutterstock: 2 (SnapASkyline), 4L (Vector Illusion), 4R (Nickolai Repnitskii), 5 (lev radin), 8 (Dmitry Rukhlenko), 10 (Andrew Park), 11T (Arjun bna), 18 (Suvendu Das India), 19 (Rahul Sapra), 23 (Tyshchenko Photography); Superstock: 11T (Amit Somvanshi), 11B (Zohaib Hussain), 15T (Hermes Images).

British Library Cataloguing in Publication Data (CIP) is available for this title.

ISBN 978-1-78856-214-0

www.rubytuesdaybooks.com

Contents

Words shown in bold in the text are explained in the glossary.

This Is Our Faith

The faith of Sikhism began about 500 years ago.

People who follow this faith are called Sikhs.

This **symbol** is Ik Onkar.

The words "Ik Onkar" mean "there is only one God".

A Sikh family in India

Sikhs believe in one God who created all living things.

A kind, wise man named **Guru** Nanak was the **founder** of Sikhism.

Sikhs in New York worshipping at a temple, called a **Gurdwara**.

"Sikhs call God Waheguru, which means "Wonderful Teacher" or "Wonderful Lord". Sikhs believe that all people are equal. God loves everyone the same."

"When Sikhs worship, they sit on the floor to show that everyone is equal and they are all part of the same community. No one is more important than anyone else."

Sikhism began in a place called the Punjab. This region is now split between India and Pakistan. Today, Sikhs live all over the world.

The Life of Guru Nanak

Guru Nanak was the first of ten Sikh gurus, or teachers.

Nanak was born in 1469 to a Hindu family. He studied Hinduism and Islam and thought deeply about faith.

A 200-year-old painting

The birth of Nanak

A 300-year-old painting

Rescuers looking for Nanak

Nanak underwater

Sikhs believe that one day Nanak was bathing in a river and disappeared underwater!

His family thought he had drowned. But after three days, Nanak returned home.

While Nanak was gone, God came to him and shared many important lessons.

- There is one God for everyone.

- People should live every day with God in their hearts.

- All people are equal.

- People should share with others and serve others.

- People should be honest and kind.

Nanak began to share God's message with others.

He became Guru Nanak and his teachings became a new faith called Sikhism.

Before Guru Nanak died, he chose one of his followers to become the second guru.

Sikhs making free food to share with people at a parade

The Guru Granth Sahib

For the next 200 years, one guru followed another.

The Sikh gurus wrote down their teachings, prayers and hymns.

They created a **sacred** book called the **Guru Granth Sahib**.

The first-ever version of the book was written by the first five gurus. It was placed in the Golden Temple at Amritsar, in India, in 1604.

The Golden Temple at Amritsar

"You might hear Sikhs call our **holy** book the "Shree Guru Granth Sahib". The word "Shree" is a way to show **respect** and devotion."

Each of the ten gurus added to the sacred text.

A wise, Sikh teacher called a Gyani.

The Guru Granth Sahib

Every copy of the Guru Granth Sahib has 1430 pages and contains exactly the same words.

Finally, Guru Gobind Singh, the tenth guru, said there would be no more human gurus after him.

The Guru Granth Sahib would become the **eternal**, living guru.

"The Guru Granth Sahib is the living word of God. It gives me all the answers I need. It's like having a kind, wise teacher with me when I read it."

The Forming of the Khalsa

Guru Gobind Singh was the tenth and final guru.

In 1699, he created a special community of Sikhs called the **Khalsa**.

Members of the Khalsa promise to be brave, to stand up for what is right and to live good lives.

Today, many men and women still become Khalsa Sikhs.

Hundreds of years ago, Khalsa Sikhs were warriors who defended their faith against enemies. Today, some Sikhs carry swords at ceremonies and parades. The swords are not weapons, but symbols to show their history.

Turban

Symbolic sword

Kara bracelet

These men are Khalsa Sikhs.

Kara

A circular metal bracelet. Its shape is a reminder that God's love has no beginning and no end.

Kesh

Long, uncut hair to show you accept God's will. A turban is worn to keep the hair tidy.

Kanga

A small wooden comb to keep the hair clean and tidy. It is tucked into the hair.

Kirpan

A short, curved dagger. It is worn hidden away and is a symbol of protection of the Sikh faith.

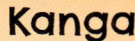

> Members of the Khalsa wear five special things at all times to remind them of their promises and their faith. These things are called the Five Ks.

Kachera

Plain white shorts worn as underwear.

> Many Sikhs choose to wear a turban even if they are not members of the Khalsa.

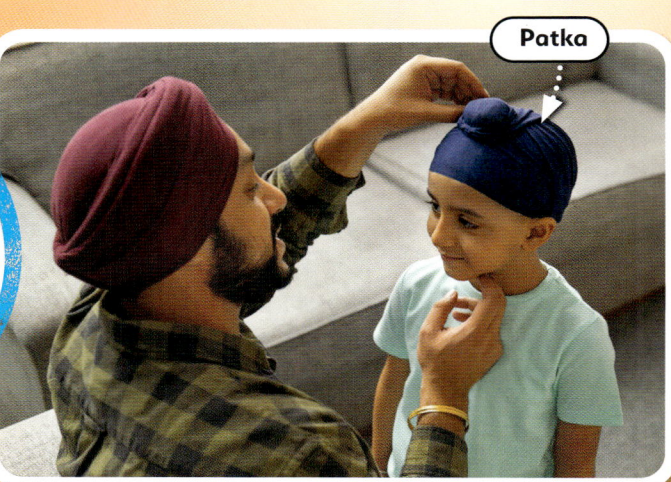

Patka

> Sikh boys keep their hair long because it is a gift from God. They wear a small piece of cloth called a patka to keep it tidy and safe.

Welcome to a Gurdwara

Sikhs worship at a temple called a Gurdwara.

In the prayer hall, worshippers pray before the Guru Granth Sahib.

A Gurdwara in Kent, in the UK

The book is gently fanned to show love and respect.

Granthi

Cloth-covered Guru Granth Sahib

When it is not being read, the holy book is covered by a beautiful cloth to show respect.

A special Sikh teacher called a Granthi reads and takes care of the Guru Granth Sahib.

The Guru Granth Sahib is placed on a special platform called Manji Sahib.

Worshippers pray, listen to teachings and sing hymns called kirtan.

Manji Sahib

A Granthi puts the Guru Granth Sahib to rest at night.

After worship, everyone eats some sweet pudding called Karah Parshad. Sharing this treat shows everyone is equal and **blessed**.

It's Time to Share Langar

After worship at a Gurdwara, everyone shares a free, vegetarian meal called **langar**.

Every day, food is prepared in the Gurdwara's langar kitchen.

A langar kitchen in India

Anyone can come to a Gurdwara to enjoy langar. It is one of the ways that Sikhs share with others.

Volunteers serving langar

Serving others without expecting anything in return is called seva.

A langar meal in London

Men, women and children all **volunteer** to cook, serve the food and clean up.

Everyone eats together, sitting on the floor in the langar hall.

" Sometimes langar food is donated to food banks. Sikhs also give money to charities. Helping and showing love for others is a way to show love for God. "

Let's Celebrate! Gurpurab

In November, Sikhs celebrate the birthday of the first guru with the festival of Guru Nanak Gurpurab.

Before the festival begins, the complete Guru Granth Sahib is read out loud at all Gurdwaras.

This special reading of the Guru Granth Sahib is called Akhand. It lasts for two days and two nights. A team of people share the reading so it never stops.

A Gurdwara in Pakistan

People visit their gurdwaras to listen and to pray.

On the day of Guru Nanak's birthday, many communities have a parade called Nagar Kirtan.

The Guru Granth Sahib is carried with great respect through the streets on a float.

A Nagar Kirtan parade

The Guru Granth Sahib

People sweeping ahead of the float in Leicester, UK

Nagar Kirtan means "singing songs through the town". The Sikh community walks together singing songs for God.

People sweep the roads ahead of the Guru Granth Sahib to make them clean and respectful.

Let's Celebrate! Vaisakhi

In April, the joyful spring festival of Vaisakhi takes place.

Sikhs celebrate their faith and the beginning of the Khalsa.

Most Nagar Kirtan parades are led by five Khalsa Sikhs dressed as the Panj Pyare. They are a reminder of the first-ever five members of the Khalsa.

The Panj Pyare means the "Five Beloved Ones".

Sikhs visit their Gurdwaras, enjoy Nagar Kirtan parades and share special meals with family and friends.

At the Vaisakhi celebrations there are exciting displays of dancing and Sikh martial arts.

Sikh martial arts called Gatka

During Vaisakhi, some Sikhs become new members of the Khalsa. At a ceremony, they promise to be brave, kind and honest. They also promise to wear the five Ks at all times.

Many people wear **traditional** clothes at Vaisakhi and for the Nagar Kirtan parades.

Naming a New Baby

Soon after a new baby is born, their family takes them to the Gurdwara.

The baby is presented to the Guru Granth Sahib.

A new baby boy is given the surname Singh, which means "Lion". A baby girl takes the surname Kaur, which means "Princess".

The Granthi opens the Guru Granth Sahib at a random page.

The first letter at the top of the left-hand page will be the first letter of the baby's name.

Guru Granth Sahib

Granthi

Worshippers share Karah Parshad from the same bowl. This shows everyone is equal and part of the community.

Karah Parshad

The family chooses a name and everyone says prayers.

Then the family and other worshippers share sweet, holy Karah Parshad.

Welcome to a Sikh Wedding

A Sikh wedding ceremony usually takes place in a Gurdwara.

The bride and groom bow and sit before the Guru Granth Sahib.

Bride and groom bowing

A Granthi or important member of the community says prayers and talks about the couple's life together.

Next, is a part of the ceremony called the Lavans.

There are four Lavans, or hymns, and each has a special meaning.

As each hymn is sung, the couple makes one slow walk around the Guru Granth Sahib.

Each hymn and walk is like a special promise to walk through life together with love, kindness and God's blessing.

This bride is following a Punjabi tradition. She is holding the groom's sash as they walk.

"After the ceremony, everyone eats langar together. Then later, there may be a big party with more food, music and dancing!"

GLOSSARY

blessed
To be given and to receive God's protection and love.

eternal
Lasting forever.

founder
The person who starts or sets something up for the first time.

Gurdwara
A building where Sikhs come together to worship and spend time as a community.

guru
A teacher who shares wisdom and helps guide others.

Guru Granth Sahib
The holy book of Sikhism. Sikhs respect the Guru Granth Sahib as their living Guru and follow its guidance for life.

holy
Very special and important, and connected to God.

Khalsa
A special community of Sikhs who have promised to live truthful, brave and caring lives. They wear five special items, the five Ks, at all times as reminders of their promises and faith.

langar
A vegetarian meal that is cooked in gurdwaras and shared for free with all worshippers and visitors.

respect
Acting in a kind, careful and polite way to show that a person, place, object or belief is important to you.

sacred
Something that is special or holy. It is usually important because it is connected to God.

symbol
Something that stands for something else – for example, a heart shape is a symbol for love.

traditional
Something that people have been doing for a long time, such as celebrating a particular festival or wearing clothes connected to their culture.

volunteer
To offer to do something without expecting anything in return. Also, the word for a person who volunteers.

INDEX

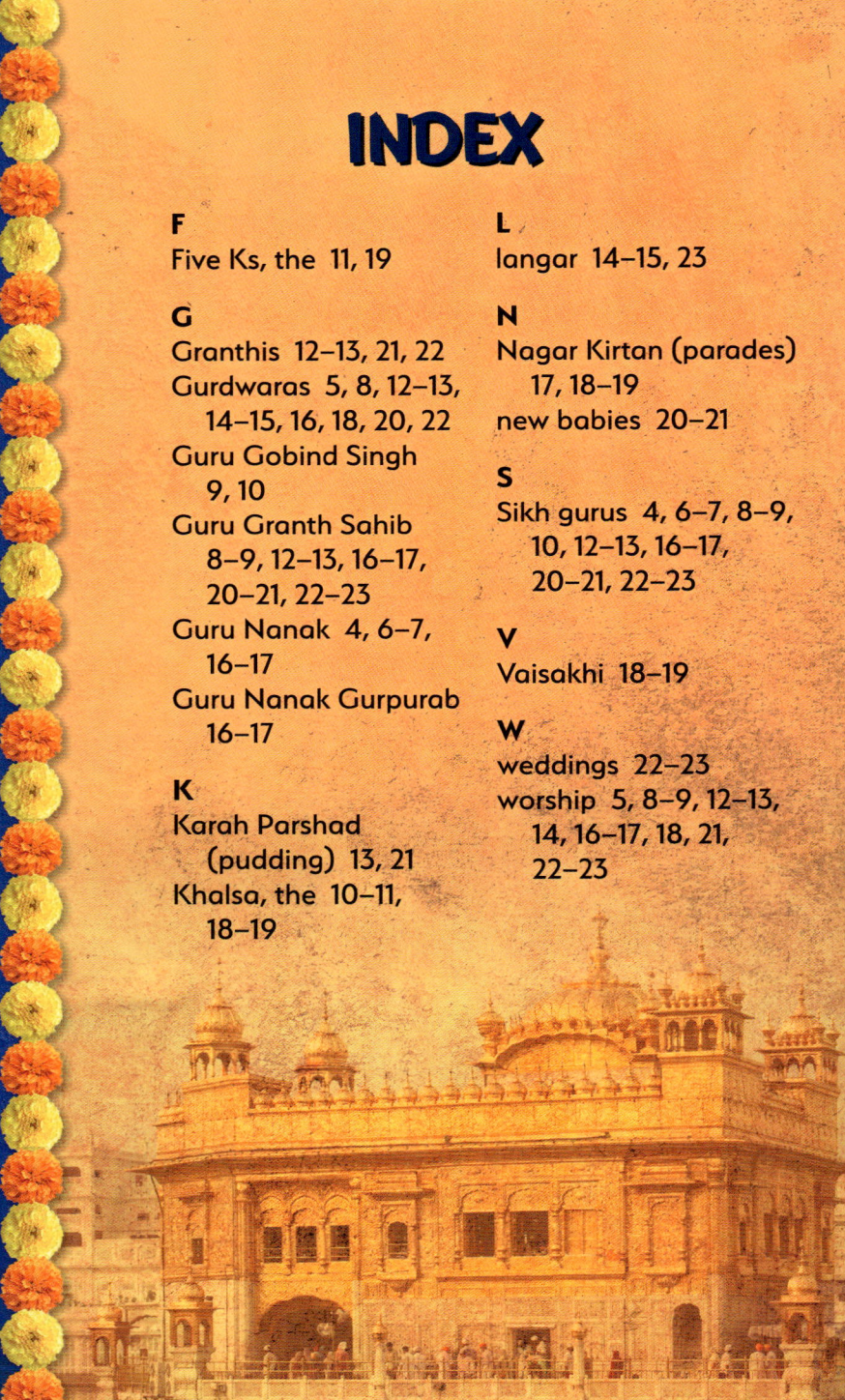